Advance praise for Cartoon E

"Dr. Hoekstra has illuminated a mindful approach to psychological suffering, incorporating current best practices with a captivating cartoon book showing us exactly how it's done."
--Beth Brownlow, M.D., Psychiatrist, Concord, Massachusetts.

"In this thoughtful, sensitive, and humorously illustrated guide, Dr. Renee Hoekstra distills years of clinical experience in working with clients who struggle with painful emotions into a compendium of step-by-step guidelines for dealing with one's unwanted emotions with acceptance and wisdom, compassion and hope."
--Mavis Tsai, Ph.D., Co-Developer of Functional Analytic Psychotherapy, Independent Practice and University of Washington, Seattle, Washington.

"With *The Emotional Extremist's User's Guide to Handling Cartoon Elephants*, Renee Hoekstra has constructed a charming and accessible allegory that addresses painful and challenging material in a fresh and friendly light. A lovingly-illustrated travel guide to bring on safari through one's own darkest jungles, the Guide takes the reader's hand and gently but firmly leads an expedition toward the pursuit of any missing, hypoxic, or stampeding Extreme Emotions (in the guise of adorable but formidable cartoon elephants). Deceptively whimsical, the book's nuanced layers invite the audience to read and re-read the material, to be revisited alone or with a travel companion such as a partner or therapist. While most readers will recognize elements of themselves in these pages, the book will be especially appealing and relatable to people who struggle to corral intense emotions, and to those who provide treatment or support to such individuals. A great book to ponder alone or with a therapist, Dr. Hoekstra's graphic novel provides a gentle introduction to the confrontation and resolution of painful emotions."
--Michelle L. Imber, Ph.D., ABPP, Clinical Neuropsychologist, Boston, Massachusetts.

"Rarely does one find a book that is both whimsical and practical- especially one that deals with the world of difficult feelings. In this book, Dr. Hoekstra manages to use humor and fun to help people run toward and not away from feelings that keep people stuck, in pain, and acting in ways that hurt themselves and others. Recognizing and managing feelings can make life much easier for ourselves and those around us. Whether it is people suffering from and acting out their early trauma, or those who just need some help understanding the way they feel and act and why, this wonderful new book can clarify what is happening and show the way to a less painful life. "
--Leisl Rockart, Ph.D., Psychologist in Private Practice, Boston, Massachusetts.

"This book is an intelligent and entertaining guide concerning day-by-day mental hurdles. It is a gentle approach for many of our emotional responses to challenges. With humor, prose, and illustration Dr. Hoekstra helps fill the void by visualizing ways to address the obstacles of everyday life."
---Dr. Jeremiah DiRuzzo, D.C., Chiropractor, Boston, Massachusetts.

"Renee reveals herself to be a master elephant handler–and she's ready to teach you to be one, as well! *The Emotional Extremist's Guide to Handling Cartoon Elephants* is not simply fun and engaging, it's emminently useful for all of us, and really, it's all of us who must learn how to handle the cartoon elephants that inflate their way into our lives or pop up at inconvenient moments. Don't let the rhinos discourage you from picking up this book!"
--Matthew D. Skinta, Ph.D., Clinical Health Psychologist & Researcher, San Francisco, California.

"Dr. Renee Hoekstra's *The Emotional Extremist's Guide to Handling Cartoon Elephants* is just what is says. This is a delightfully illustrated book that helps the reader learn to directly observe, without fear or attachment, the 'biggest problems in the room'–extreme and sometimes out-of-control emotions–and with calm acceptance, bring them down to size. Her cartoon elephants teach cognitive self-management skills directly and comfortably. Without realizing it, while reading, I found myself becoming aware of my current state, watching distractions come and go, and...just breathing! This book is a humorous, caring way to teach principles and techniques to manage intense emotional states. I highly recommend 'Cartoon Elephants' for self-help and for therapists trying to teach such skills in a relaxed and thoroughly engaging style."
--Gordon Herz, Ph.D., Psychologist in Private Practice, Madison, Wisconsin.

"With her creative and playful cartoon elephants, Hoekstra communicates complicated lessons about emotions and emotional well-being. Both interesting and easy to remember, her elephant stories reframe our emotional experiences and suggest new solutions to emotional problems. I highly recommend this fun and engaging book to anyone wanting a new perspective on emotions and how to better manage them."
--Christy Matta, M.A., Therapist, Trainer, and Author, Sunnyvale, California.

"Renee Hoekstra's book is a gem. Inviting, direct, funny, full of profound wisdom and practical advice, this deceptively simple little book can help you live a fuller life. Many books claim to help you better control your emotions. Based on the most recent developments in evidence-based therapies, this one gently shows you how to make your peace with the turmoil and invite your emotions to join you in creating the life you want."
--Benjamin Schoendorff M.A., M.Sc., Therapist and Author, Montreal, Quebec.

"This book explains, in an engaging and whimsical manner, practical ways to deal with the difficult and painful feelings that get in our way. This charming illustrated guide helps us recognize, name, and manage the emotions that hurt us, hurt others, and keep us stuck. It helps the reader move away from self-blame and guilt and gives practical advice that is actually based on current best practices of cognitive therapy. It is a simple and friendly approach to what can sometimes be experienced as complicated and difficult to learn. This book will appeal to people of any age who are trying to develop a more mindful approach to dealing with their emotions."
--Rebecca Walters, M.S., LMHC, LCAT, TEP, Hudson Valley Psychodrama Institute, Highland, New York.

Dear Reader: If you have ever

- Been trapped or stuck in an emotion
- Had extreme, unwanted, or painful emotions
- Had missing emotions
- Found yourself unable to figure out what to do with your emotions
- Been confused by emotions
- Not known when to let go of emotions
- Been unable to allow your emotions sufficient oxygen
- Been unable to separate your emotions from criticism
- Needed more control of your emotions

THEN

You need this book.

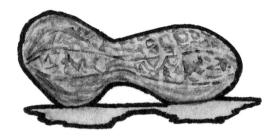

The Emotional Extremist's Guide to

Handling Cartoon Elephants

How to solve elephantine emotional problems without getting run over, chased, flattened, squished, or abandoned by your true cartoons.

Renee Hoekstra, Psy.D.

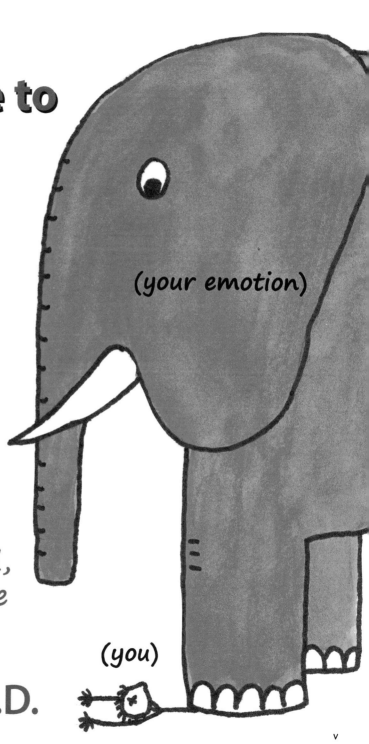

(your emotion)

(you)

Contents

Part I: The problems of cartoon elephants ....page 1

The non-existence of cartoon elephants.....................................*page 4*
The weight of cartoon elephants..*page 10*
The equilibrium of cartoon elephants..*page 13*
Stampeding, out-of-control elephant situations..........................*page 17*

Part II: The basic steps for solving elephantine problems...................page 23

Part III: When your cartoon elephants are in danger: How to cope with critical obstacles..page 67

Part IV: When solving elephantine problems seems impossible: What to do when stuck beneath an elephant's foot...page 83

Part V: What to do when elephants end up on your back.....................page 101

Part VI: What to do when your cartoon elephant turns blue.............page 111

References:..page 131

Part I

The problems of cartoon elephants

Everyone has cartoon elephants.

Emotions

At times, you may have found yourself believing that cartoon elephants

DO NOT EXIST.

"There aren't any elephants in this room...."

BE YE NOT FOOLED.

Cartoon elephants do, indeed, exist.

There is research to prove it (Acrtnrhno, 2007; Acrtnrhno, 2008; Bigphant & Liliphant, 2011; Hoekstra, 2012; Hoekstra 2013; Masses, 2009; Phant & Oiliphant, 2012; Skin and Serious, 2011).

HOWEVER,

It is possible that you have

IGNORED

your cartoon elephants for

SO LONG

that you have fooled other people into thinking that elephants

DO NOT EXIST.

SO I am going to tell you a very short and simple

story

about someone
who worked very
hard to

ignore elephants.

Beginning:

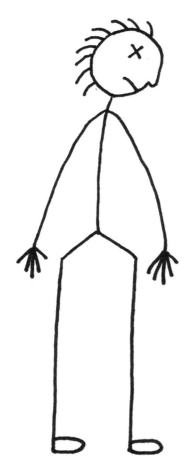

Middle:

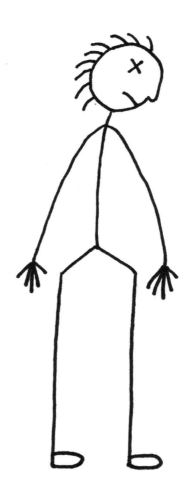

End:

Did you notice a *plot line?*

(Neither did I.) If you are a person without a plot line, you are in

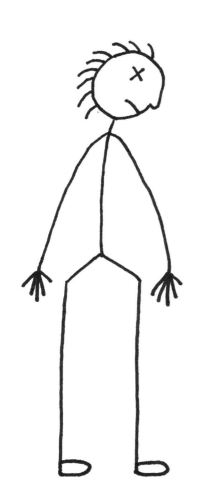

BIG
TROUBLE.

"But I am fine."

LOST: ME

Myself.
My energy.
My vitality.
My life.

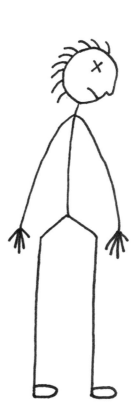

Sometimes,

if you look very closely,
you may discover that
cartoon elephants
have **NOT**, indeed,

Gone

Missing.

THEY HAVE ACTUALLY BEEN THERE ALL ALONG.

11

LOST:

Power.
Hope.
What matters.

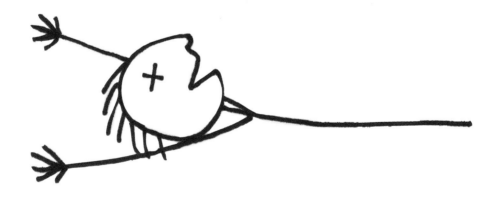

You may have spent your

ENTIRE LIFE

in the spin cycle
of the
washing machine
with your
cartoon elephants....

Going around...
and around....

and around....
       and around....

LOST: All

Equilibrium.

Of course, we can't forget about stampeding, out-of- CONTROL elephant situations...

LOST:

All control

Whatsoever.

Part II
The basics for solving elephantine problems

FIRST, Try to find out which elephants are in the room with you. You may not succeed immediately.

Keep trying.

DON'T GIVE UP.

Take notes if needed.

As you can

(or cannot)

See,

an ignored elephant is not a visible elephant.

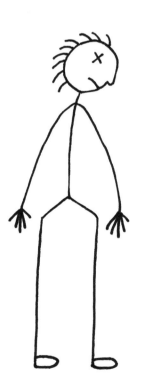

GO YE THEREFORE AND FIND YOUR ELEPHANTS.

DO NOT BE AFRAID OF

what you discover.
If you find yourself
running away from your elephants,
you will have to find out

what

you are running away
from.

FIRST,
stop running.

NEXT,
turn around.

STOP

waving
your
hands.

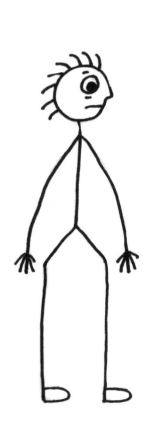

Put your
arms
down.

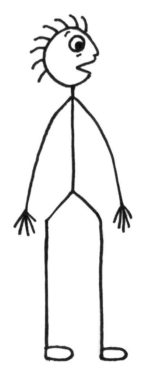

Close
your
mouth.

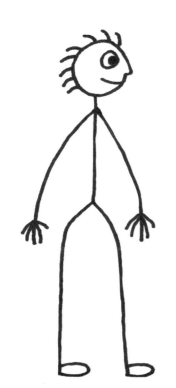

MOST IMPORTANT,

gently relax
your face.

Once you turn around
and start looking

at your elephants,

you may find that they bunch up

like a bad traffic jam.

FEAR NOT.

You are going to experience the **flotsam**

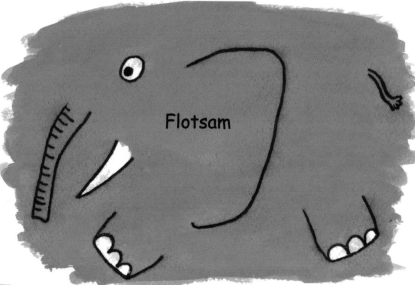

and **jetsam** of cartoon elephants

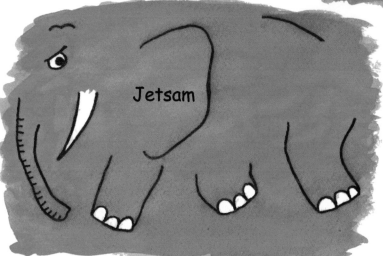

from time to time.

It is important that you keep your facial expression soft and your gaze curious.

- Drop your shoulders
- Unclench your jaw
- Wriggle your fingers
- Relax your pelvis
- Lengthen your exhale

Practice loose and floppy.

This will allow you to get in touch with your true cartoons.

Once you get in touch with your true cartoons

you will have to sort out

Sad

what is what,

Irritated

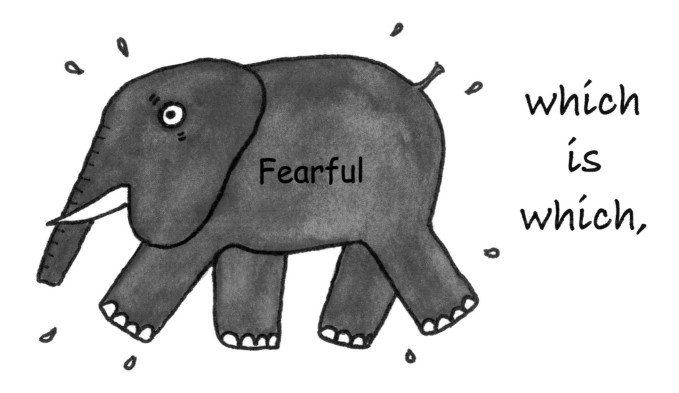

which
is
which,

Fearful

and
who
is
who.

Resentful

Keeping in mind that when you sort through your elephants,

you will have to pay

the most attention

to what comes **FIRST**

Pain of
sadness

and much less attention

to
what
comes
second

Angry
because you
don't like
being sad

or
even
what
comes
third.

Guilty
because you
are angry that
you are sad

NEXT, Gather as much information

as *possible* on all the reasons cartoon elephants exist.

First of all, DO NOT:

- put your hands on your hips
- scrunch up your forehead
- tighten your facial muscles

and demand:

WHAT GOOD ARE YOU?

Try softening your shoulders, standing up straight, facing your elephant, and asking directly,

"What might you be trying to tell me?"

Try pulling up a chair and making yourself comfortable. Cartoon elephants will actually give you important information if you listen willingly.

"Do you know that your own fears keep you from getting what you want? You avoid the things you want the most! You do care! You are afraid of showing the world who you really are."

Sometimes cartoon elephants are *working very hard* to get you to solve a painful situation.

"Taking action is necessary but HARD!"

"Do what needs to be done!"

"If you don't get moving, things are going to FALL APART!"

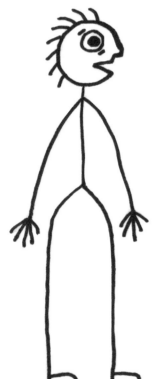

"GET GOING!"

Sometimes they are encouraging
you to take a risk on love.
"I want to tell you how much
our relationship means to me."

If you pay very close attention,
you may also receive
an invitation.

Do not ignore the invitation!

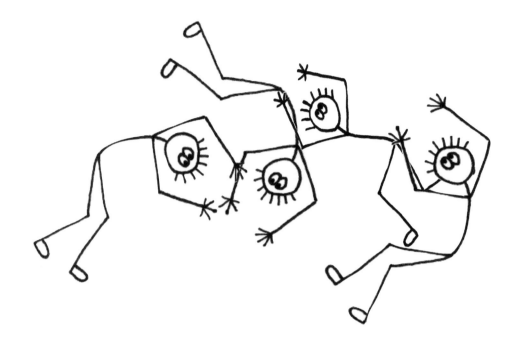

When your
elephant
pulls you in close
and invites
you
to sit
on his back

You may be overwhelmed with the magnitude of what is at hand. **DO NOT** try to get out of it. It will be very important to figure out how to **GUIDE** your elephant.

It is entirely possible that
your elephant won't know
what to do with you once he's got
you on his back...
and will
make
a
run
for the
BOONIES.

It is very important for you to understand that cartoon elephants do not run to the boonies with

ILL INTENTIONS.

They are just doing what cartoon elephants do.

And they need your help.

Examples of what **NOT** to do when your elephant is taking you to the boonies:

- Throw your hands up.
- Scream loudly.
- Roll your eyes wildly back and forth in your head.
- Lose your posture.

TAKE NOTES HERE:

Your elephant is looking for your guidance.

You will need to step up to the plate.

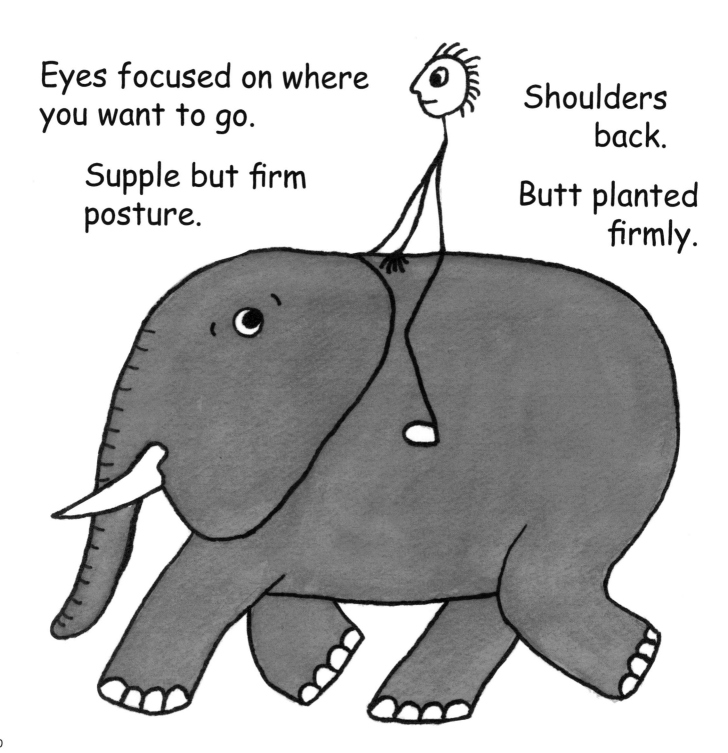

Eyes focused on where you want to go.

Supple but firm posture.

Shoulders back.

Butt planted firmly.

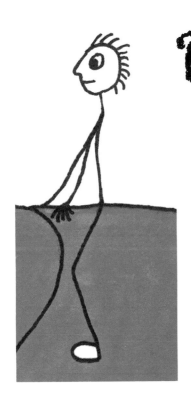

Practice FIRM, flexible, and confident

without becoming

STIFF AND RIGID.

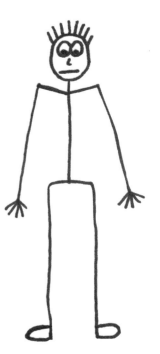

But
dont
forget
that
you

will also
need to practice

loose and floppy

without

becoming

spineless

Because
When you are
able to do both
flexibly, your
CARTOON
ELEPHANTS

will start
to take
you to the

PLACES
YOU INTEND
TO GO.

Sometimes *this will come easily.*

But mostly

IT WILL NOT.

Overview of the basics:

- Find missing elephants.
- Look at your elephants (the gentle yet curious gaze).
- Practice loose and floppy.
- Sort and identify elephants.
- Gather information on the reasons cartoon elephants exist.
- Listen carefully to what your cartoon elephant is telling you.
- Guide runaway elephants.
- Practice firm, flexible, and confident.

These steps may take

Multiple Repetitions and Multiple Reminders.

Repeat them often.

Part III

When your cartoon elephants are in danger: How to cope with critical obstacles

Sometimes in your
search for cartoon elephants,

you might come across a few

CARTOON
RHINOCEROSES

DO NOT MISTAKE

YOUR cartoon elephants

for *cartoon rhinoceroses.*

Like real rhinoceroses,

cartoon rhinoceroses
have poor eyesight

and like to attack

ANYTHING

THAT MOVES.

"Feelings are a BIG WASTE OF ENERGY! *Why can't you get over yourself and move on?*"

"*Feelings are stupid!*"

"Obviously no one else feels the way you do."

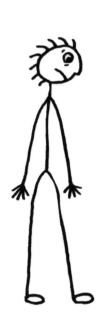

"Why do you always have to make a big deal *out of nothing?*"

"YOU SHOULDN'T FEEL *that way.*"

"Plaster a SMILE on YOUR face and act STRONG."

71

While you might be inclined to

pretend rhinos

ARGUE

agree

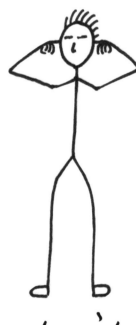

don't exist

disagree

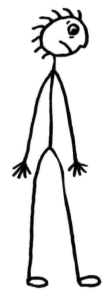

look down

These responses

will probably

NOT

help you solve the

problems

of cartoon rhinos.

Instead, **KEEP LOOKING** for your elephants.

Gently acknowledge your rhino and walk right on by.

"I see you standing there. But I wasn't looking for *YOU*."

You may find your cartoon rhinos to be **relentless.**

Be equally persistent.

"I'm sorry that you are having so much difficulty believing in the existence of cartoon elephants.

Clearly they exist or they would not leave tracks!

Perhaps you'd like to join me in my quest instead of standing in the way."

STAY
FOCUSED
ON THE
TASK
AT HAND.

You should
find that

when you steadily

PERSIST

on your cartoon-
elephant
quest

The magnitude
of your rhinoceros-sized
problems will, over time,
shrink in size.
The truth is,
cartoon rhinoceroses

WILL

SHOW UP

from time to time
throughout your life.

NEVER STOP BELIEVING

in the existence of your cartoon elephants.

NO MATTER WHAT.

Part IV

When solving elephantine problems seems impossible: What to do when stuck beneath an elephant's foot.

First of all, **DO NOT GLARE.** Fighting your elephant will only result in *ongoing injury.*

Your elephant will be most receptive to your influence when **YOU** are receptive to your elephant.

Take a
moment
to
notice
**the change
in your
elephant**
when you
GLARE

And
when
you
do
not
GLARE.

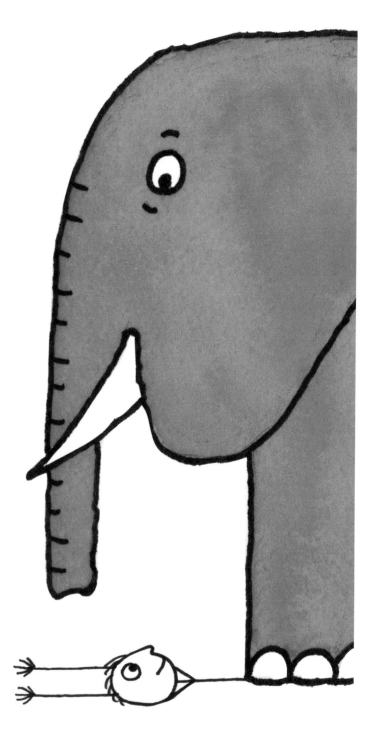

Granted, if you are stuck beneath an elephant's foot, the

Last thing

you will want to do is

Stop glaring.

(In fact, it may seem

DOWNRIGHT COUNTER-INTUITIVE.)

When you stop glaring,
you may still be
inclined to
proceed with

TREPIDATION.

Instead, consider
approaching
this
situation with

CURIOSITY.

Gently observe what
your elephant
is up to.

Respect
his
presence.

Follow
his
movements.

Track
the heaviness of
his weight.

When you create

as many
open
invitations
as possible
for your elephant
to be assured
that you are no
longer at war,

Your elephant will no longer see you as a threat.

You will will start to become an expert in noticing

subtle
changes
in
elephantine
SHIFTS OF
WEIGHT.

FULLY EXPERIENCE

what it's like when you encounter an abundance of wiggle room.

While these steps will **NOT** *rid* you of the elephants in your life

(THAT BECOME elephantine),

They will give you options to influence

where your elephant puts his feet

when
he
starts
to
loom
all
around.

Part V

What to do when elephants end up on your back.

When you focus your attention on everything **EXCEPT** your cartoon elephants,

strange things
start
to
happen.

For instance, you may be walking around with blue cartoon elephants on your back

without even noticing.

Take a moment to
LOOK AT
what is *actually* going on here:

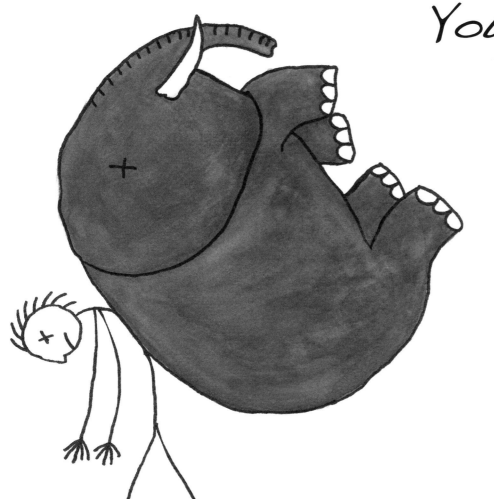

You, unable to see

WHAT,

exactly,

you have been carrying around

all these years.

Some people have even carried their
cartoon elephants on their backs all the way
across the Himalayas*

*Himalayas not drawn to size

If you listen very, very closely, you may be able to discern what is actually being said:

"My pain is worse than your pain and you could never understand how I feel so get lost things will never change stop trying to tell me things are different life sucks and this is awful and if you are trying to convince me otherwise it is proof that you cannot understand my situation so I will forever be lonely and miserable and I will work extra hard in order to prove to you that you are wrong and that I cannot be helped I am perfectly fine hauling my elephants over the Himalayas day after day after day and I am not tired or exhausted at all I can do everything by myself I am fine I don't need anyone or anybody to help I am not vulnerable and I never need things from other people so get out of my way I don't care how mean or lonely or tired I sound I just have to keep going and going and going if I bite your head off because you tried to help me don't be surprised but you might keep trying and I will keep biting your head off and my whole life will be lived like this and I will be okay just fine and dandy remember I'm okay this is horrible and I can't stand it but remember leave me alone because I just have to keep getting my elephants across all these mountains I could never ever ask for help let me be..."

HOWEVER,

this

may be somewhat

exhausting.

PROS of keeping elephants on your back:

- Justified suffering
- Avoidance of painful realities
- Strengthened belief that chronic back pain builds character
- No risk for rejection

CONS of keeping elephants on your back:

- Chronic sore back
- Loneliness and alienation
- Troubled relationships
- Lack of intimacy
- Forever invisible

SET THAT CARTOON ELEPHANT DOWN!

He will not like being dumped on his rump.

(But things will change.)

Stand up straight. Bring your shoulders back.

INHALE
SLOWLY
AND
DEEPLY.

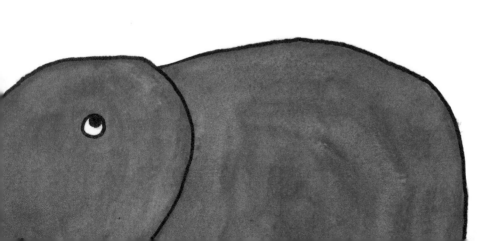

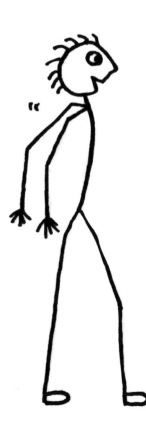

Once you are standing up straight you will (of course) have to turn around and **pay attention** to your elephant.

Part VI

What to do when your cartoon elephant turns blue

If you have been **carrying** your elephant across the Himalayas, you may find your elephant to be Unrecognizable.

Oxygen- deprived elephants need oxygen
STAT.

Tips for proper oxygen administration:

Inhale when you **pull up.**
Exhale when you **push down.**

Steady.
Even.
Consistent.

Try making eye contact with your elephant.

Inhale,

exhale.

If distractions happen,
simply
return to the breath.
DON'T GIVE UP.

119

When you finally get enough air into your elephant, make sure you take a

Good long pause in order to

fully experience

Interacting with your elephant in a way that

Feels Good.

You may find that (sometimes)
even though you've given your
elephant **OXYGEN**
Your cartoon elephant may
have changed.

It will be important for you to know that there are simply times when cartoon elephants are ready to move on.

LET CARTOON ELEPHANTS GO when they are ready.

When you say goodbye to old elephants,
remember that new ones

will never be very far behind.

Greet each
new
elephant gently...

...and willingly let your elephant go when the time comes.

As you do this more and more, you should find the whole cartoon elephant experience much, much easier.

Remember to always accept your cartoon elephant just as he is,

In the current moment he is in,

How-
ever
he
shows
up in
your
life,

And to
let
him go
when the
time
comes.

Once you understand the basic art of cartoon elephant maintenance, your elephants will become much less threatening and much easier to relate to.

Cartoon elephants will **ALWAYS** be part of your life,

For better or for worse,

Clear or unclear,

Big or small.

And if you stay in touch with your cartoon elephants...

You too,
will be touched
by them.

References*

Acrtnrhno, R.U. (2008). The day the world looked at cartoon rhinoceroses and lost sight of elephants: Increased measures of psychological distress. *International Journal of Cartoon Pachyderm Research, 20,* 82-103.

Acrtnrhno, R.U. (2007). Pachyderm psychometrics: How to increase your chances of obtaining true positives and true negatives when measuring elephantine situations. *Journal of Cartoon Psychometrics, 16,* 36-51.

Bigphant, L. & Lilphant, E. (2011). Summary of documented blue cartoon elephant sightings in the Himalayas: Does anyone know what we are really looking at? *South Asian Journal of Cartoon Pachyderms, 4(4),* 44-61.

Hoekstra, R. (2012). A healthy pink glow: Differences in cartoon elephant colors as a measure of emotional wellbeing. In Phant, L.E (Ed.), *Elephants of a different color: How to determine if true cartoons are really true.* (pp. 19-27). Boston: Pachyderm Publishing Company.

Hoekstra, R. (2013). ACT, FAP, DBT, and MBCT: The prevalence of pink pachyderms in alphabet soup. *Journal of Cartoon Psychotherapy Integration, 14,* 12-27.

Masses, T.H.E. (2009). How to determine cartoon elephant intensity based on color, size, and speed. In Phant, L.E. (Ed.), *Elephants of a different color: How to determine if true cartoons are really true.* (pp. 54-71). Boston: Pachyderm Publishing Company.

Phant, L.E. & Oiliphant, O. (2012). Who made it all the way to Mount Everest with cartoon elephants on their back? Three case studies ending in complete and total disaster. *South Asian Journal of Cartoon Pachyderms, 8(1),* 86-123.

Skin, Th. K. & Serious, B.N.G. (2011). Face validity of the Inventory of Existing Cartoon Elephants (IECE). In Pyngattention, R.U. (Ed.). *Annual mental measurement yearbook of cartoon pachyderms* (pp. 200-226). Boston: Pachyderm Publishing Company.

*These fictional studies have been published in fictional journals and fictional books using fictional research and fictional pachyderms.

How to get the most out of this book

- Read it over and over again. Try to figure out what else you can get out of the book every time you read it.

- If something in the book is puzzling, try to find someone who will give you his or her interpretation of it.

- Talk about this book with the important people in your life.

- Start discussions about what this book means to you.

- Identify what resonates with you, what is familiar, what stands out, and what applies to you.

- Tell other people to read it.

- Show this book to the people in your life who don't talk about emotions.

- Use this book to start a conversation about emotions. Start the conversation by sharing how the book applies to you. Then see if the other person might be willing to share how the book applies to him or her.

- Buy this book and give it as a gift to the people you think need it the most.

Make sure to visit
www.cartoonelephantbook.com

CPSIA information can be obtained
at www.ICGtesting.com
Printed in the USA
LVIW02n0838140813
347803LV00003B